I Just Need a Helping Hand...

and then I'm Going to Make It!

I Just Need A Helping Hand... And Then I'm Going To Make It!

Script Marker
500 8th Avenue FRNT 3 #1560
Manhattan, NY, 10018
(516) 684 9243
www.Script-Marker.com

ISBN 979-8-89523-016-9 (Paperback)
ISBN 979-8-89523-017-6 (E-book)

Printed in the United States of America.

I Just Need a Helping Hand...

and then I'm Going to Make It!

Joelle Lewis

Contents

Unblock Your Power To Get What You Want!

Change your life with a life skills toolbox!

Joelle's new book details the steps towards total transformation and regeneration: physical, emotional, mental, and spiritual.

The life-skill tools in this book will empower you to move from victim to victor and to turn tragedy into triumph. Whether your problem is one of unhappy relationships, illness, career choice, or simply general dissatisfaction, you will find in these pages the answers to your most personal questions.

Learn tools and methods that can help you:

- understand exhaustion and resentment
- overcome despair and depression
- increase your understanding and awareness
- raise your self-esteem and self-confidence
- heal and improve your relationships
- achieve your desired goals

Joelle says, "I learned everything the hard way, but I learned it well. I believe that nothing can stop you from living the life you want, if you only know how and why you are not doing it already. I hope the tools in my books can help you, my friends and fellow travellers, to live a completely fulfilled life and know the greatest healing and happiness in the process."

So now you know what to do with life's lemons; trade them for something you like better!

Dear Friend,

If you feel that the time is right for a change, if life is unsatisfying or not the joyous and fulfilling experience it should be, perhaps I can help you.

I have hit rock bottom in every area of my life at some stage- all at the same time more than once and recovered. I have been through some devastating experiences! Not only have I survived these, but I have become empowered by them. In this book, I want to share what I learned and how I achieved transformation and regeneration from wounded to healed, from powerless to empowered, from sad and despairing to peaceful, thankful, and joyful.

This book is what I call my "life skills toolbox." It is my guidebook to truth, wholeness, and freedom. I hope that you find it helpful in your journey.

You can read the whole book or simply open it to any page when you are troubled, and there will be your answer.

I wish you love, success, happiness, and fulfilment in all that you wish to be and wish to do with your life experience.

May God bless you and help you on your way.

Love, Joelle

This book is for all of us who wish for fulfillment.
With thanks to Nick, who woke me up.

Acknowledgements

Now that I am also a parent, I first want to thank my parents. I also want to thank the beautiful souls who are my friends for their help, teachings, and support, which have blessed my life and given me so much of themselves.

Especially-Kate, for her fun and good sense; Ray and Ber, for their empathy and faith in me, as well as their lovely Irish positivism; Agnes, for her counseling, editing, empathy, and encouragement; Carlos, for the synchronicity and confirmation; Chris, for his support and objectivity; Graham, for his enthusiasm and confidence in me; Peter and Mark, for their understanding; Ali, for his deliverance; Brett, for being a lucky charm; and all of them for their unconditional acceptance of me.

I could not have become the person I am without these people and others in my life and my heart.

I would also like to thank the universe for the learning experiences in which I have been privileged to participate, and those others who were a part of the experiences.

God bless, and thank you all.

Dedication

The night is drawing to an end,
And day is nearly here-
It's just that murky predawn time,
When things are not quite clear.
The veils are lifting slowly;
This one's the next to last-
And as it passes from my sight,
A door shuts on my past.
For now I face the future.
The sun is shining bright;
Would you move a little to the left?
You're standing in my light.

-Joelle Lewis

Life Is a Journey of Discovery

You are an adventurer, a pioneer!
No one has ever lived your life before,
nor will they again.
Every moment is a once-in-a-lifetime experience!

Sometimes, in order to value life fully,
we need the experience of dissatisfaction,
even illness or accident,
to jolt us out of a previous pattern of behaviour
that was not serving our best interests.
If we heed the message within these experiences,
we will then make necessary changes
to ourselves and our lives.

We have both an inner and an outer world,
containing unexplored territory, infinite riches,
and treasures beyond measure.
We have so much living,
being, and doing to experience!
Activate the explorer within yourself;
animate your interest
in the myriad possibilities for experiencing life.
Get fascinated by the world out there
and within you,
and choose to make your life
a gloriously satisfying experience.

Make your life an adventure you'll enjoy!

Why Am I Not Where I Want to Be Now?

Do your expectations reflect your true desires?
Have you set goals that will result in your personal fulfillment,
or are they to please someone else?

When we define clearly
what constitutes fulfillment for us,
we have a clear target.
Once we have a clear target,
we can easily take aim and fire!

When we find we aren't really motivated
to achieve a goal we've set,
it's generally because that goal
will please someone else but not us.
We each have our own desire,
our gift, our talent, our mission here
on Earth-sometimes more than one.
If you hate being a banker,
if you find your university classes don't engross you,
if you don't like your job,
it means you're probably on the wrong track.
You may also find
that something you once enjoyed
no longer thrills you; it may be time to move on.
Don't be afraid of changing your life;choose what pleases you.
The life you really want
is just around the next corner; aim for fulfillment!

Choose your future to really please you!

Recovery

There is always hope and scope for improvement.
Whatever your problem or situation,
you can recover, rediscover, rebuild, reinvent.

When we feel we have hit rock bottom,
when we want to give up or give in,
when we can't take anymore and we've had enough,
we are actually poised on the brink of succeeding!
You can choose to turn the light on yourself,
or to wait for dawn but there will be light either way.
So it is with the end of our dark moments as well.

Often, we put off acknowledging
our need for change until it is long overdue.
Begin with small steps to do something about it.
The first step towards positive change
is to acknowledge the need for that change.

When we find ourselves fed up
with the way things are,
this is the turning point
when we will take action
to effect change for the better.
We make the decision
to do something about our problem,
and we take positive action
towards the life we want.

We are now setting out on the road to recovery.

Understand Beliefs

Our beliefs shape our world.
Whatever we believe, it will be so for us.
If we believe that we are clumsy or undeserving,
then that will be our world.

Conversely, if we believe we are worthy,
deserving, capable, and acceptable,
then that will be our world.
What sort of world do you want to live in-remembering that it is only
your beliefs that need to change
in order for your whole world to change?
It matters not what others think;
what you think
is what makes the difference for you.
You cannot be teased, insulted,
belittled, or humiliated
unless you believe
that what is being said about you is true.
You are whatever you believe yourself to be.

So how do we begin to change our beliefs?
The tools in this book
will help you question and reassess your beliefs,
to understand where they came from
and how to change them
to something that works better for you,
freeing you to be the best you can be!

Our beliefs about ourselves
govern our thoughts, our actions,
and our interactions with others.
Changing our beliefs will change our world.

You Have the Power

You are the controller of your life-once you
become aware and fully understand this, you can change
whatever is not the way you want it.

When you were a child,
you were dependent on others to provide for you,
and you were basically at their mercy.
You were less able to choose the influences in your life.

Now that you are an adult, your life is your own,
and the choices are endless. You are the creator of your life.

If you don't like something about yourself,
your job, your relationships, or your life,
you are free to take steps to change it.
You may need to take a class, move house,
hange jobs, or find new friends,
but you can do it if it's what you want.
You are the power in your own life.
Exercise that power by taking steps that move you towards your
happiness, your desires, and your goals.

Reclaim your power, reclaim yourself and your life.
It is yours to do with as you wish.
You have the power to fulfil your desires.

Happiness Is Your Birthright

We learn unhappiness; it is not our natural state.
As babies, we assumed we were okay,
until someone told us by words or deeds
that we were not okay.
At that point, we may have started to wonder.

Newly arrived in a strange land,
with little or no power of discernment,
we believed what others told us
or showed us about ourselves.
Not all babies are immediately welcomed
by their families.
The new baby may bring financial hardship
or restraint or the loss of freedom;
either way, the birth of a baby
means big change
that is not always welcomed unrestrainedly.
This is not any reflection on you personally
and should never be interpreted as such.

Whatever your beginnings,
your family circumstances or upbringing,
you are here because you are meant to be here.
You are here because the universe wants you to be.
See the bigger picture.
The whole world is your home and your true family.

You are always a wanted child
in a bountiful and benign universe.
Happiness is your birthright.
Know this to be true, and act on it.

Miracles Abound

We are surrounded by the miraculous:
the air we breathe, the sun that shines,
the flowers and trees that grow,
and the rain that refreshes.

Children are born and grow;
broken bones and hearts mend;
ailments are cured;
new technologies are invented,
and new relationships formed.
Look around you
and see the miracles everywhere, every day.

Within us lie even more miracles.
We breathe, we think, we feel;
our skin renews, our blood pumps;
our hair grows, our muscles move us around.
Every cell in our body is renewed regularly.
When you focus on the miraculous,
any changes you want to make
can be seen as possible and attainable.
You can grow bigger, smaller,
younger, different, better in any way you wish.
You control your body,
and you can choose to treat it well or poorly.
Learn how your body works;
learn its rhythms and its needs.
Listen to your body.
It will tell you everything you need to know
about whatever's wrong with you.

It's up to you how you grow and renew!

Give Thanks for Your Life

Be grateful for the gift of life.
Not every soul gets the chance to be here;
some do, but for a very short time.
You are here because you deserve the gift of life.
Therefore, you also deserve happiness.

Count your blessings.
Look for other things you can be grateful for.
Do you have a roof over your head?
A Job? Family? Friends? Health? Talent?
Some will have more than you,
and some will have less.
It matters not what you have;
it's what you do with it that counts.
Be grateful that you are here at all.
In being here, you have choices about what to do,
who to be, and where to be.

When you desire change, you must be that change. Change your
actions, your words, and your thoughts to something that will more
positively move you in the direction you want to go.
Give thanks for those things you do have.
Focus on the good in your life, in the world,
and then imagine better.
Giving thanks for what we have and are given ensures that
we are given more.

Gratitude helps us grow in love.

You Are Already There

You have everything you need within you now
to be whoever or whatever you want to be!
You may also have within you a lot of blocks, negative views, and hang-
ups preventing you from achieving your dreams.

Often they are the result of years of conditioning
by society, culture, and family.
Our beliefs about ourselves
also came from our own childhood reactions
to events and influences,
from interacting with
other people's unresolved wounds and problems. Sometimes even a
chance remark by someone else is enough to set us back.
We don't have to accept what others say about us
or the way they treat us as being the truth about us.

Like digging for buried treasure,
obstructions need to be removed
to reveal your true self in all its glory.
The purpose of the obstructions was once protective.
It is now safe and necessary to remove them, to find, heal, reveal, and
free the real you.

Transcend Limits and Limitations

Think of all the barriers that have been broken
by those who don't accept limits on achievements.

The three-minute mile, crossing the ocean,
flight, the space race, computers,
organ transplants, and so on.
People everywhere are doing things
others said couldn't be done!

What a wonderful thing to do-
something others said couldn't be done!
Wouldn't you feel wonderful if you did something, anything that
someone said could never happen? Have you done anything wonderful
yet that you previously thought you couldn't?

Do it!
Transcend the belief in limitations of any kind,
and go for your dream.
Give it everything you've got,
and never doubt for a moment
the possibility that it can happen.
Do it for you!
Anything can happen, anywhere, anytime.
Why not make that work for you
by imagining what you want to happen for you. There really are no
limits to what you can achieve, except those in which you believe.

Develop Enthusiasm

Nothing will change for you unless you change.
The hardest part of getting out of a rut
or getting off your butt
is taking the first step!

Motivate yourself
with enthusiasm for what you want.
Inspire yourself to achieve your goals and desires. Take a walk, get a
study buddy, read inspirational books, watch inspiring movies, talk
with others, ask for help, pray, sing, dance, listen to rousing music, or
rub yourself all over with a rough towel.
Do what you must. Get that blood flowing.
Get that body moving. Get those eyes sparkling. Get that mouth smiling.
Strut your stuff!

Up and at it!
Nothing is going to drop into your lap;
you are going to have to do something
to bring about change.
Brainstorm your problem with creative thought.
Can you go over or under it, around or through? There is more than
one solution for any problem. Begin, and it will soon be done.
Believe in yourself, have courage, and persevere.
Trust in the best possible outcome, believe that you can and will
succeed in your endeavours.
You are more than a match for any problem!

Write Your Recipe for Life

In a journal,
set out your headings
for each area of your life:
How would you describe you, as you want to be?
What are your dreams for your career?
What do you seek in a relationship?
Who is your perfect partner?
What sort of lifestyle do you crave?
What are your ideal living arrangements?
What qualities do you treasure in a friend?
Where would you take your dream holiday?
And anything else you can think of.

Use pictures (either drawn or cut out of magazines), words, and
colours to illustrate your ideals for each.
Be as specific as you can.
Describe yourself and your life
as you would want it to be.
What would happen if your most cherished,
and deeply desired dreams and dearest wishes came true?
Note a date on your entries,
and don't be afraid to change your mind
as often as you like.
Your wants, needs, and desires
will change as you grow.
This is as it should be.
We can change our goals and set new ones.
We can have short-term and long-term goals.

The universe really does want you to have everything you want,
so ask for what would fulfil you,
enable you to feel happy,
and make you supremely content
at every stage of your life.

Dream big, completely fulfilling dreams!

You Are Perfect

In the great scheme of things,
you are always perfect
just the way you are
at any given time.

Whoever, whatever, and wherever you are now
is a stage in your journey.
You don't have to stay that way forever,
but you can if you want to.

You may want to change something
about yourself or your life,
and that's what this book is about.
It is important to first accept yourself
totally as you are now.
Learn to love and accept who you are
at every stage of your journey.
We are human beings,
all God's children born of woman,
yet we are different from each other.
Our individuality is what makes us
so interesting and loveable.
To find and express the best of your being
is the path of growth to success,
happiness, and fulfilment.

You will always be you,
even as you change and grow.
If you don't love you,
you won't believe that anyone else can or will.

Give yourself your unconditional acceptance.
Your foibles and individual traits
are what make you-
a unique and unrepeatable being.

Expect a Positive Outcome

*Sometimes we sabotage our own best efforts
for positive change by worrying
about what could go wrong.
We limit our own potential
when we surrender to the fear
that whatever can go wrong, will.*

*Nothing in life is all smooth sailing.
Even if you stay where you are,
the way you are now,
you will still have problems and issues to deal with;
that is not going to change.
In all probability,
none of us will ever have a life
that is free of any problems!*

*Maybe you are just used to worrying
because you've had time to worry.
Make yourself too busy or too mellow instead.
If it's going to happen,
it'll be something you haven't thought of anyway!
Focus on the best possible outcome, give up worrying, and spend your
time getting, doing, being, having, and enjoying what you really want
to be or do.
You can deal with anything that comes up
more easily if you remember
that you are on your way
to who and where you want to be.*

*Remember that
often the things that can go right
will go right.
Yee-ha!*

Think, Speak, and Act Positively

If it's not already your habit,
practice thinking and speaking of yourself,
and others, events, and experiences
in positive terms.

Look for and find the positive
in everyone and everything.
It is possible to choose what we say and think.
For example, "She has a vibrant personality"
is so much more positively focused
than "Her clothes were not ironed."
Aim to help yourself and others feel good.
"I have lovely hair" is more positive than
"I don't like my fat bottom."

Every experience can be seen in a positive light. Rain is not depressing,
it's refreshing! Your partner didn't leave you
because there was something wrong with you;
it was because
you were not the right one for him or her.

By changing our words,
we change our thoughts and vice versa.
When you focus on the positive
and think and speak positively,
your whole world will change.

You'll find yourself becoming
the sort of person people just love to be around.
You'll like yourself better too!

Attract Your Good

Focus on the good and on the best outcome.
Describe it in detail, and feel it intensely!
Once you decide, either it will come to you
or you will be drawn to it.

When you are focused in this way,
whatever comes to you
will be a step in the right direction.
It may be unclear to you at the time
exactly how this is so, but have faith.
You are still steering your ship,
and the universe is helping you
to your goals.

Our end goals and desires
do not always manifest instantaneously.
Sometimes we are not ready for them;
perhaps not quite seasoned or experienced enough.
Don't be disappointed in the waiting;
rather, determine to enjoy the anticipation
and the journey to the attainment of your goals.

Every stage of our lives is a necessary part
of the process of growth.
Our good will always come to us
if we stay focused on it.
At the same time,
it is also often necessary
for us to grow into our good,
so we can release any restrictions and limitations,
preventing us from accepting and keeping it.

Eliminate Criticism

As we begin the process
of accepting and loving ourselves
the way we are now,
we will find the things about ourselves
that we can't accept and we hide.

If we were to see ourselves
through the eyes of our Creator,
we would see the perfection of our individuality.
We are given unconditional acceptance and love by our Creator,
so why do we find it so hard
to give this to ourselves?

Look carefully at the criticisms
you have of yourself.
Ask yourself if they are helpful.
If others have tried to make you feel inadequate
in some way,
they were probably feeling that way themselves. Some people put
others down so they can feel superior.
Advertisers want you to buy their product,
so they're going to tell you you'll fail without it.
Use your discernment
and take it all with a pinch of salt.

Understanding that others
tell you things or do things to you
because of their own problems or agendas
helps you to release their opinion of you.

Practise and expect acceptance, not judgement.

Break Old Patterns

*The influence of years of conditioning
is not easily overcome.
Willingness to change is good,
but then we need to put it into action.
It's time to take the first step.*

*Start now.
Do something differently.
Begin to break old patterns and habits.
If you usually drink tea with milk, try it black. Rearrange your furniture. Change
your hairstyle. Do something right now
that will give you a taste for change!
Then keep it up.
Go to work a different way.
Be untidy. Be neat.
Try on different personalities.
Be different in any ways or areas
of your life as you wish.*

*Changing little things in your daily life
will help you break old patterns and habits
and give you a taste of change
without having dire consequences.*

*Try joining a drama group
or play act different roles,
just as you pretended
to be Batman or Wonder Woman
when you were a child.
Dress up as someone else.
Wear a disguise.
Pretend!*

Be creative. Be flexible. Loosen up.

Get a taste for change.

Change is good fun!

Right Action, Right Thinking

What's right for you is the right thing to do.
When we practice right action,
right thinking will follow you
like a faithful shadow and vice versa.

When you know what you want
and are quite clear about it,
your actions will naturally take you there.
Also, by acting as if, we can change our thinking.
Choose whichever method works best for you.

Sometimes, we get what we want,
only to find we didn't really want it after all.
When we practice right thinking,
our choices are made by our higher selves,
the wise part of us that knows
what would really fullfil us,
regardless of societal or family pressures.
Choose what pleases you
in partners, jobs, and lifestyle.
The "perfect" one is the one that's perfect for you.
Decisions motivated by concern
for the opinion of others
will leave you an empty shell,
all for show to others
but lacking the substance
that would enrich and fulfil you.

When you are truly fulfilled
and enriched by your choices,
you have mastered the art of integrating
right action and right thinking.

Practise Effective Communication

We can change the way we are treated by others.

Our own fears and frustrations
can cause us to bring out less than the best in others,
just as theirs can put us on edge.
When we want to communicate our displeasure
or frustration with another,
we often end up scolding, blaming,
and making them wrong.

By communicating our position effectively,
we can elicit better treatment from others,
and also show them how to get the best from us.

Rather than resorting to blaming others,
own your frustration.
First, try to explain the problem:

"When you say or do ... I feel..."

Next, state your desire: "I would like you to be..."

Finally, make it clear what you want.
Don't be afraid to be specific
when sharing your suggestions:
"In future, would you please say or do ..."

By reversing the position of I and you
in the above conversation,
and restating what others say to you,
you can also help them
to improve their communication.

When we more effectively communicate our desires,
we are more likely to have them fulfilled.

Affirm, Confirm, and Make Firm

Your words have energy.
The strength of your words
not only helps you make things come true,
it allows the universal energy to help you too.

Affirmations can be spoken, chanted or sung,
but they are always positive
and in the present tense.
"I now have the perfect job, partner, and life."
"Only the best for me comes to me now!"

Use them for your own growth as well.
"I am now confident, healthy, happy, and successful."

This is a fabulous way
to reprogram your thinking about the new you.
It is also a powerful way to overcome
the old criticisms that were holding you back before.

Go ahead! Create your own affirmations!
For example, if you are held back by shyness,
your affirmation could be,
"I now meet people confidently and easily."

Affirmations confirm and make firm
the changes you want
as though they had already happened,
so make your affirmations
according to the recipe you wrote earlier.

Understanding Cause and Effect

*Our problems are mostly caused
by our relationships with others.*

*Our problems are also mostly healed
by our relationships with others.*

*Choose consciously the company you keep,
in as much as you are able, given your awareness and
experience at the time.
Often relationships that challenge us
turn out to be good for us in the long run
because they provide an opportunity
to heal our wounds.
They allow us to face our limitations and delusions,
to change previous patterns
which were detrimental to our best interests,
to learn about ourselves.
And even though it may be a painful lesson to learn, by showing us
what we don't want, relationships can also teach us
what we do truly desire.*

*When you are with people, learn to become aware
of the effect and influence each has on you.
Choose your influences, role models, and mentors according to who and
what you want to be. At the same time,
be aware of your influence on others around you.*

*Choose those who influence you positively.
Resolve to be a positive influence on others.*

Be Your Own Best Friend

The one person
best able to have your best interests at heart
at any given time, in any situation
is you!

Feelings of disappointment,
betrayal, victimisation, humiliation,
resentment, martyrdom, and so on
remind us that we were expecting another
to put our interests before their own.
We must be realistic in competitive situations.
However, this is not a licence
to trample over others.
Rather, this should be viewed as an acceptance
of the outcome as a learning experience
from which we may gain either way.

You are the best friend you will ever have,
so treat yourself accordingly with love, acceptance, kindness,
consideration, and respect.
Learn your strengths and weaknesses.
Cultivate your talents and skills.
Know your needs and wants.
Grow into the sort of person
you would want your best friend to be.
Be someone you can love and admire.

How we treat others
is a reflection of what we think of ourselves.
Empower yourself with self-love,
self-acceptance, self-confidence, self-respect.
Know that you make the biggest difference
in your life.

Liberate Your Spirit!

We are often trapped, captured,
lured, or seduced by baits and tempting enticements which seem to
offer easy solutions
and trouble-free paths.

We are pressured to conform to collective norms,
to change our round-peg self to fit a square hole,
to merge with the majority,
and maintain the rigid status quo.
We become enslaved rather than liberated,
calcified instead of creative.
We must be true to ourselves in order to truly live.
This means we must have the strength to know
what is right for us
and the power to hold to that conviction.
We must develop courage, tenacity, and perseverance,
for often individuality is a battle we will fight
against those who would have it otherwise.

Be real!
Choose wisely and well.
Choose your partner, your work, and your life path
to nourish your spirit
and to support, explore, and develop yourself.
Refuse to live your life as a slave,
caged for the benefit of others.

Be true to you!
Uphold your inalienable right to your own life
and your own self-expression.

Understand the Purpose of Pain

Pain is our stop indicator,
a valuable tool
that tells us when we are no longer working
in our best interests.

Physical pain
tells us that something is wrong with our body. Emotional pain
tells us that we have issues we are resisting. Suppressing emotional
pain can lead to physical symptoms of disease.

There is no shame
in freely acknowledging and seeking treatment for physical pain,
so why let yourself feel shame
when you feel equally torturous emotional pain?
We would not continue on painkillers
while leaving a broken leg unset,
yet we often leave our emotional wounds
festering freely while we dull our pain
with alcohol and tranquillisers.
We also leave ourselves open
to repeat the wounding.
Freedom from any pain
comes from accepting it as an effect
and taking action to cure its cause.
The first step is always to relax, rather than resist.
You are not your emotions or your body.
Detach or seek assistance
so that you can clearly identify the problem
and seek the cure.

When you empower yourself to face your issues,
you can deal with them openly.
You can then choose to heal your wounds fully.

Feel It, then Heal It

You can control how you act.
You can control how you feel.
You can control how you handle your own life.
You can't control others.
You can't control events.

You can choose
to concentrate on healing your own emotions.

You can choose
to control your own actions and reactions.

Observe and accept your feelings-
they are telling you where your pain is.
Acknowledge pain as the doorbell to the room of understanding.
Talk about the issue with a friend or counsellor.
Write about it in your journal.
Heal the wounds within you properly
with kindness and love.
Ask what the pain is trying to tell you.
You can then heal and grow through understanding.
When someone or something pokes your wounds,
don't take it out on them; breathe it through.
Take deep, slow breaths in and out.
They have done you a favour
by showing you where you can be hurt.
We can only be hurt when we don't understand
or when we focus on protecting ourselves
from hurt instead of healing it.

Get in Touch with Yourself

After a lifetime of denial and repression of our real selves,
how do we get in touch with our feelings?
Humming a song, drawing a picture,
or writing a poem
are good ways to access buried feelings.

As we become better able to access our feelings,
we experience more of life.
When we are able to express our negative feelings, we
become free to express our positive feelings.
By not denying feelings of anger,
sadness, pain, and grief,
we are more able to fully feel
joy, happiness, calm, and peace.
So express your feelings!
Cry, wail, punch a pillow, or spend a day in bed.
When you free yourself to feel,
you free yourself to heal.
Your laughter and smiles
will be less constrained too.
The ritual of wailing at funerals
in European cultures is very healthy.
Our feelings are normal human traits
that need expression.

Get in touch with your senses as well.
Wear silk, roll in the grass, eat with your fingers,
smell flowers, drink in the beauty of nature,
bathe in bubbles, play music,
sing, dance, dream, and love.

When you connect with yourself,
you connect with life.
Open yourself fully to experiencing life.

Understand Harmony and Teamwork

There you are, playing your guitar solo.
Along comes someone with a piano,
drums, and so on.
In this way, we each have a contribution to make.
Each part contributes to the whole and makes it
more beautiful and meaningful.

This is teamwork.
There are many combinations
that work well together... and some that don't.
Some work well as a quartet but not a duo.
A guitar goes well with a banjo or drums,
but not as well with a trombone, for example.
Define your desired music
and choose your players accordingly.
When we are looking for harmony,
we need different but complementary players,
not so much more of exactly the same,
but rather those who will harmonise
well with us.

Harmony is resonance.
When we are looking for partners,
friends, or team members,
we need to seek resonance and cohesion.
Resonance comes from complementary qualities.

Cohesion comes from similar values,
a shared interest, or a common goal.

We are all instruments in the orchestra of life.
The quality of the music depends
on how well we each play
and how well we play together.

Overcome Unfamiliarity

Sometimes, even though we want change,
we choose to cling to the old way.
After all, it's safe. It's comfortable. It's familiar.
The unknown can be quite scary, even threatening.

Do you remember the teddy bear
or security blanket you had as a child?
Do you remember how scary big changes were
when you were small?
Things like the first day of school,
moving to a new house, or as an adult,
the uncertainty of starting a new job
can all be cause for anxiety.
Remember how scary that was at first.
Even positive changes,
like taking steps to make healthier choices,
can feel unfamiliar and strange at first.
You haven't yet learned how to live with it.
You aren't used to the new experience yet.

Know that it is completely normal to be scared.
It's perfectly normal to be uncomfortable at first.
Take comfort in knowing that these feelings will pass.
Very soon, the new will become known and familiar.
So persevere with the changes you want to make
to yourself and your life.
Hold firmly to your vision of the new you.

Soon enough, it will be true.

Overcome the Resistance of Others

*You may find that your problem with change
is that those around you resist it.
They want you to stay the same
because it's comfortable ... for them!*

*If we want to change our habits,
our behaviour, our lives, we are free to do so.
We learn by making mistakes,
correcting those mistakes, and moving on.
We are not our mistakes.
Neither are we our behaviour;
it is only a form of expression
that we are free to change.
Don't stay the same to please others.
Life is the path of growth towards wholeness,
not stagnation!*

*Hold firm to your resolve.
Your first duty is to yourself.
Only your own happiness
is directly within your power to create,
maintain, or destroy.
In order to maintain the status quo
(which is probably serving their interests
better than yours),
others may try to control and manipulate you
in various ways.
This is often done unconsciously,
so realise that they may need time
to get used to the new you as well.*

*Remember,
no one has the right
to ask you to live for their sake.
Our lives are our own to live as we wish,
in peace and harmony with our world.*

Reflect Your Environment

We are influenced by our environment,
and it may not be the one of our choice.
The easiest way to effect change then
is to change our environment
to one that better reflects who we really are,
or who we want to become.

By travelling, reading books, seeing movies,
and so forth, we can visit different worlds,
evaluate different ways of life,
and experience different ways of being.

A hopeless, drab environment can drag us down.
Yet without moving,
we can change that particular environment
by the use of colour, plants, music, laughter,
and other creative solutions.

We can also use change of environment
to our advantage in other ways.
If you burn to become a lawyer
but are surrounded by builders,
try frequenting the coffee shops
where lawyers hang out
or visit the public gallery at the courts.

Search for or create
a nurturing, encouraging environment
to support the changes you want to make
to yourself and your life.

Reflect Others

Often we find it hard to go against the grain.
Why?
We have been raised a certain way.
We have been in a groove too long.
We don't know what's possible.

Especially if we have come from a background
of abuse, poverty, or neglect,
it can be difficult to imagine
exactly what the ideal is.
We only know what it definitely isn't!

So much of what we learn is by repetition.
We tend to emulate what has been role-modelled
for us by the significant people in our lives.
To some extent,
we are all mirrors for those around us...
so choose your mirrors consciously.

Finding mentors who will work with us
and who are positive role models
is an excellent way of learning
the skills we need in order to make the transition
into our new lives.

Workshops, classes, support groups,
friends, and our heroes from the past and present can help us to meet
this need.

Once you have your blueprint
-your model of all the desirable qualities you admire-
you can simply begin to act
as if you are already who you want to be.

Stretch

Stretch!
Stretch your body and your mind.
Stretch the limits of your understanding.
Stretch the limits of your knowledge.
Stretch the limits of your life experience.
And most importantly,
stretch the limits of your capacity for enjoyment.

Start by stretching your body.
Even if you're running late,
make time for a big stretch.
Yawn when you get up every morning.
This is a practice that will improve your whole day
and therefore your life.
You'll be more relaxed, alert, and positive.
You'll be physically fitter!
Stretching yourself improves your posture
by straightening you upright.
When you are physically upright,
everything follows.
Your thoughts lift naturally,
you become more positive,
and your eyes are now focused straight ahead.
Furthermore,
when you commit to starting your day calmly,
you will cope better with the day's challenges.
You'll gain the confidence
to deal with whatever comes your way,
calmly and without any overreaction
caused by an accumulation of stress.

Continue stretching your capacity
in other areas of your life.
Seek to boost
your compassion and understanding for others.
Work to increase your curiosity
for subjects that interest you.
Stretch your skills at home, at work, and at play.
Stretch your whole experience
of every minute of your life.

Relax

Many of us are unable to truly relax
without feeling guilty.
Too many of us feel that there is always
something we should be doing instead!

Nothing in life was ever made better by rushing it.
Taking five to thirty minutes each day for total relaxation
will prolong your life, reduce your stress,
and allow you to recover energy and equilibrium.
Lie down flat on your back, with your feet elevated if possible.
Try clenching every muscle tightly,
before relaxing or shaking yourself like a rag doll.
Any tensions will then be released.
Try calming yourself with timed breathing.
Count slowly to five for each inhalation.
Count slowly to five for each exhalation.
Repeat until you are in a place of serenity.
Think of floating clouds or other peaceful scenes.

Setting challenging but achievable goals
for yourself will help you avoid being overwhelmed and stressed.
Prioritise tasks in order of real importance.
Remembering that perfection is not always necessary or desirable!
Delegate or enlist help from others
as an alternative to taking it all on yourself.

Relax for maximum efficiency and effectiveness.

Find Peace Without

While we are focused on achieving our goals
and striving to get where we're going,
we often forget to create balance in our lives.
Action needs to be balanced with inaction, excitement with peace.

Spend time somewhere peaceful
without distraction or noise.
Try having lunch in a park.
Take a walk in the garden.
Sit beside still water.
Relax in a hammock or rocking chair.
Take regular time out for peaceful rest.

Feed your soul with quiet reflection time.
Appreciate and enjoy the beauty of nature.
Stop to be thankful
for all of nature's many gifts,
including the air we breathe,
the colours and scents of flowers,
the cool forests, the rolling green hills,
majestic mountains, burbling water,
and joyous birdsong.
Twice each day,
nature puts on a show of breathtaking beauty
in her sunrises and sunsets.
The moon and the stars decorate the night.
The seasons and weather change to give us variety.

We are blessed with this beautiful world.
Find the ways in which you can enjoy,
cherish, and preserve that blessing for yourself
and those to come.

Find Peace Within

Conflicting thoughts and emotions
can throw the natural rhythm
and equilibrium of our internal system
out of balance.

Natural methods are our gentle ways
of bringing ourselves back to balance.
Safe, gentle, noninvasive, and effective
methods of rebalancing the emotions
for adults, children, and pets
include naturopathy, homeopathy,
flower remedies such as Bach flower
and Australian Bush flower,
aromatherapy, acupressure,
yoga, prayer, meditation, and Tai Chi.

Try music, dance, singing, massages, facials, soaking in the bath with
salts or oils, swimming, lying on the grass or sand.
Ensure you also get enough sleep.
Talk or write out your thoughts each day.
Do you keep a diary or journal?
Do you have a trusted friend or counsellor
to whom you can unburden yourself?
Talk to God or write letters and burn them.

Find peace from any internal torment
in ways which are healing and safe for yourself
and others.
Please don't kick the dog,
shout at your partner,
or physically harm anyone
in your attempts to relieve stress.

Violence only begets more violence.

Clean Out the Rubbish

In order to make room for the new,
we have to throw out the old.
Our new self with our new life
is there at the door, waiting to come in.
We want to have a home environment
which will support, encourage, and nurture this.

It's time to spring clean.
Banish the unworn clothes,
the unused items,
the unsupportive people,
and most importantly,
our outgrown habits.

After writing out our recipe,
we should have a clear picture of what we want. Anything that doesn't
reflect the new life we want and the new person we want to be should
be thrown out, recycled, sold, or given away. It has outlived its purpose
or usefulness in our lives.

The new can't come into our life
if we are so cluttered by the old
that there is no room for it!
Remember with gratitude
what you've had.
Bless the old as you part with it.
Mark the occasion with some sort of ritual or party.

The new awaits you!
Welcome it joyously!

Don't Repress It, Express It (Safely)

Sometimes, strong influences
can oppress and repress our natural self-expression,
which can depress us.

Ideally,
we want to have all our energy
available to us.
When we learn to express it
in ways that are positive and in our best interests,
we get what we want!

Have you ever felt
that your joy has been stolen from you by others? That you have chosen
to let someone repress or oppress you?
Have you ever conformed
to another's expectations of yourself?
How did that make you feel?
We may even have hated our lives
because we weren't living it
the way we wanted to.
Repression and oppression
can lead to disease and depression.

When we take steps to empower ourselves,
we reclaim our lives and access that energy.
We can then choose to express it safely in positive,
fulfilling ways such as
going after goals we want to achieve,
playing sports, or learning a new skill.

As our self-esteem, self-confidence,
and freedom of expression increase,
we are able to access all of our energy
and express it positively
so we can achieve our goals.

Clean Out Old Hates and Anger

When our pasts are unfulfilling in some way,
it's natural to find buried anger and resentment
as a result.

Anger and resentment
are normal human responses
to misunderstanding and frustration.
We may not even realize
that we have these buried feelings,
but invariably they are there.
If we have been taught that it is bad or wrong to express anger, we
tend to bury them.
Often, buried anger and resentment shows up as acne, aches, stiffness
in our joints, and worse.
Some believe that even cancer is caused
by not expressing anger effectively.

There are a number of different exercises
which are useful for expressing
anger and buried resentments.
Try taking deep breaths to calm yourself.
Try talking or writing it out.
Convert the energy into exercise or physical labour.
If you're ready to try a simple way
to release anger in a healthy and positive way, try this:

Lie down on your bed and stiffen up.
Pound your clenched fists against the bed.
Kick your legs as hard as you can.
Growl, swear, or scream as you pound,
and give vent to your frustrations, and angers.
Use your whole body;
every cell has its own memory.

Allow anger out
and those problems will disappear.

Release the Past

*Especially at times
when we are dissatisfied with life
and looking for change,
we become aware of various grudges we hold.
Do you cling to anger
over events that didn't go your way?
Things you wanted and didn't receive,
things that were done to you,
or regrets over things you did or didn't do?
These feelings are energy stealers.*

*In order to regain our energy
and enable ourselves to move forward unhindered,
we need to release our hold on them.
The first step is to consciously realize
that those events and people
served a purpose in our lives.
They showed us
that something about ourselves needed attention.
They revealed our wounds
including low self-esteem, fear, pride,
ego, or insecurity so we could heal them.
These are our problems
and therefore, our responsibilities.
Sometimes talking it over with someone who cares
is both helpful and healing.
Sometimes getting help
from a friend or counsellor
is better than suffering alone
and in silence.*

*Holding on to resentment and regret
does you more harm than good.
It has no effect on anyone else.
By doing this, you give your power away.
For your own well-being,
choose to let go
of it as soon as you can.
Choose to release yourself
and any others involved
from the anger and resentment.
Choose to be free!*

Focus on the Flame, Not the Blame

You are born an individual
with your very own character.
When you were a child,
you developed an operating system
to deal with the world around you
according to the way your personality
interacted with it.
Your survival was at stake.

As an adult,
you are now dealing with a different world.
You will need a different operating system,
maybe even upgrades
to your thinking "software"
or your personal "hardware."
As an adult,
you also know that
you are responsible for yourself and your life.
As an adult,
you are responsible
for the achievement of your desires.

Blaming your parents,
your schooling, or other people
is not going to help.
Dwelling on the past
and wishing it were different
is not going to help.
What will help?
Learn to focus on the flame of your desire instead.
What kind of person do you want to be?
What kind of life do you want to live?
Make changes now.
Nothing in the past is as important
as the present and the future you want.

Your power is in the now.
What you want to do is focus
on what will be of benefit to you now!

Understand Disease and Depression

If we were not born diseased or depressed,
there must have been a time
when we were
healthy and happy.

What changed?
When did you decide that you were feeling less
than happy and healthy?
You must have something
against which you can compare,
otherwise you would not label yourself
"un-anything."
Think back
and determine when things first changed for you.
It may have been an experience
like moving away from a known environment
or a change of life direction.
Realise that it was only your difficulty
in accepting or assimilating this change
that has brought you to your present state.

Now, with the benefit of hindsight,
determine what you could have done differently.
What could you have done to transform that experience a positive and
successful one?
How could you have dealt with it in a way
that would have made you look forward to it?
Write down all the things you can think of.

Put those plans into action.
Take those steps now!
Learn from your experiences.
Learn from your mistakes too.
Change to something
that works better
for you.

Understand Exhaustion

*Exhaustion
can be experienced as
physical, emotional, mental, or spiritual.
We feel enervated
instead of energised.*

*Exhaustion from overexertion
is generally easily corrected by rest,
but other forms of exhaustion
are more often cured by action.
We can take action
by making conscious choices, decisions,
and by setting limits.*

*Often we feel exhausted
because we feel conflicted
or because we feel we that
events or circumstances affecting us
are outside our control.
Therefore, we reason,
there is nothing we can do about it.
The truth is that we can do something!
We can choose our reaction to circumstances.
We can choose to make them work for us.
If we find ourselves immobilised,
we can accept it with grace.
Would you rather consciously choose
to spend the time doing nothing ...
or spend the time doing something interesting?
We can also choose to talk or write about it.
We can choose to change our circumstances.
We can choose to make a decision
as to what we can do.
We can choose to act on it.
We can make choices and decisions
which allow us to regain control
of our actions, thoughts, and feelings.*

The End Is Also the Beginning

Endings are necessary for new beginnings.
Change is necessary for growth.

It's healthy to look back to see how far you've come.
It's helpful to look back to see what you've learned.
Dwelling on the past,
however, will prevent you
from being present in the now
and preparing for your future.
As a society, we are focused
on attachment and ownership.
Society thus encourages us to dwell
on loss and victimisation:
periods of mourning, natural disasters,
legal trials years after the event,
claims for compensation for losses, and so on.
How much healthier would we be
if we chose to focus on what we have gained
from any experience?
In truth, we all profit from loss;
it is about learning what not to do.

For well-being,
practise an attitude of stewardship and gratitude.
Actually, we own nothing. We have the use of various things and the
company of various people.
For this, we should be grateful.
When these are taken from us,
it means they have served their purpose.
It is time for a change.

Focus on what you have gained.
Be grateful.

Honour Endings

We need helpful ways of dealing with endings
that enable us to effectively transition
between phases in our lives and development.
It is healthy

to ritualise and acknowledge periods of change
so that respect is given to both
what has gone before and what is yet to come.
When we have rites of passage,
we have guidelines and purpose
that help us focus on necessary details
involved in any change in our circumstances.
Without guidelines,
we can easily become
lost and aimless wanderers.

We can learn much from ancient cultures
and civilizations that honoured rites of passage with ritual designed to
encourage effective transitions.
They knew how to view changes positively.
You cannot effectively
put something behind you unless you lay it to rest. Give concrete form
to your feelings, your thoughts, and memories in a memorial album or
journal. Create something you can revisit in order to fully assimilate
your experience and say your farewells.

Honour changes in your life
with a ritual that comforts,
nurtures, and strengthens you.

Face Forward

Turn toward joy and happiness.
If there is unhappiness in your past,
it is behind you already.

Play with possibilities and suspend disbelief.
From those possibilities,
one will ignite your excitement.
This, in turn, creates a probability.
When you put your intention and energy behind it, that probability can
become a certainty.

Waste no time dwelling on what is already done.
Rather, focus on what you want to do from this point on.
Your past has brought you here,
but the choices you make now
will take you into your future.
Make conscious choices,
ones that will result
in your happiness and well-being.
If you no longer find fulfilment
as the result of any choices, make new ones.
Life is meant to be enjoyed!
Have fun!

Don't take things so seriously
that you forget to enjoy yourself
in those simple, guiltless pleasures
that are freely available to us all.

Laugh at yourself often.
Choose happiness.
Make enjoyment and well-being
your highest intentions.

Choose Success

Some of us fear success
because it means change.

When we are used to dealing with failure,
disappointment, and regrets,
it can be difficult to imagine
what success will mean to us.
Perhaps we fear we can't cope with success.
After all, it is very different
from what we are used to.
It will mean learning new behaviours.
It feels much easier to fail,
because we know how to deal with that!

Moving outside our comfort zone
into unfamiliar territory can set off alarms
within us, in an attempt to stop us from changing. We even resist
changes we know are for the better. We can choose to quiet these fear
alarms with kindness and understanding.
We can take smaller steps.
We can choose a different direction.
We can use the power of our own minds
to input positive thoughts
of confidence, faith, and belief in our own ability
to deal with the success of achieving our desires.

If we can learn to accept failure,
we can also learn to accept success, can't we?
Accept fulfilment as your right and reward.
We can learn any skill we wish
to achieve our desires.

Fill It Up with Love

*As you clean
out the internal and external rubbish
and accumulated gunk in yourself and your life,
you may find that, at first, your problems get worse.*

*While uncomfortable, this is good.
Whatever gunk is in there
has to come to the surface in order to come out.
This stage won't last long at all,
and afterward, you will be astonished
at the change in yourself!
It's similar to renovating the house:
You have mess everywhere
until you finish the job.*

*Well done!
You've done all the hard stuff!
Now comes the easy part.
As you make positive changes, you will start to feel better.
You will find it easier
to love yourself
and treat yourself
and others
better.*

*If you don't already do so,
take some time to pamper yourself
with good living habits,
healthy eating habits,
and regular pampering
of your body and soul.*

*Be sure to spend time with positive people
in the fresh air and great outdoors. Go to parks!
Don't just watch children playing ... join in!
Give expression to your love of life.*

Imagination Is Creation

What we can imagine, we can create!

Sometimes we can be overwhelmed
by our negative state for a variety of reasons.
It may be a feeling of loneliness or separateness.
It may be a lack of acceptance,
continual criticism, or apathy.
It may be the belief that we are completely sunk,
with no relief in sight.

You can help yourself
by using your imagination as an aid.
Invent an imaginary friend or partner.
Imagine a personal trainer who is always available.
Invest this person with all the qualities
that would help you.
Make them positive, encouraging, accepting,
loving, kind, caring,
strong, and capable.
Anytime you feel the need for help,
ask for it from your imaginary friend.
Imagine them giving you a big hug, a kind word, powerful
encouragement, and a helping hand.
Imagine the circumstances you want.
Imagine your simple meal is a gourmet feast.
Imagine your humble abode as a palace.

Imagine yourself in the situation
you want in every detail.

Use your imagination
to create help for positive change!

Colour Your World

Our world is filled with glorious colours!
Nature surrounds us with a virtual kaleidoscope of colours,
both subtle, and strong.

Consider using colour to assist you
in lifting yourself out of
low moods and sluggish ruts.
Colour can also calm and relax you.
Soothing and supportive colours
include
pinks, peaches, apricots, and warm tans.

Earthy colours,
such as
ochre and terracotta,
are stabilising.

Uplifting colours
include
yellows, oranges, and mauves.

Cool colours,
including
soft greens and blues,
have a calming effect.

To introduce the colours you need
into your environment,
try visualising yourself
bathed in a particular colour.
Try flowers, paint, coloured paper, clothing, cushion covers, and
posters for an immediate change of environment.
You can also utilise nature's offerings
by sitting next to water, lying on the grass,
visiting the botanic gardens,
digging in the garden,
and watching sunsets.

Colour is a very effective therapy tool.

Music Is Colour for Your Ears!

Music also has a profound effect on our psyche.
It can be arousing, soothing,
uplifting, and nurturing.

By choosing music carefully,
we can alter our moods according to our desires.
Recent studies are exploring the positive effect
of Mozart's music as a treatment
for disturbed children and young adults.
Complex musical arrangements
are commercially available to help heal the damage caused by various
emotional traumas.
It is also scientifically proposed
that listening to classical music
increases one's intelligence.

Whatever is absorbed by our senses
is processed by our brains,
and thus,
affects us consciously or unconsciously.
If we allow
our intuition, our higher selves, to guide us,
we can choose wisely what we allow to influence us.
By experimenting consciously,
you will soon determine the effects of
various types of music on you.
With that knowledge,
you can then consciously choose
which is beneficial to you
at any given time.

Pray

Pray regularly.
Prayer allows us to unburden our woes
without judgement.
Prayer frees us to move on to better things.
Prayer is a very powerful spiritual tool
for change and transformation.

When we pray,
we are talking to the God within us,
as well as the universal God without.
While we cannot have
that which is not meant for us
in the great scheme of things,
we often prevent and limit the receiving of our own good
by refusing to believe in its possibility.
Prayer can help us overcome this resistance.
Prayer encourages us towards change and growth.
It is a vehicle by which our soul can tell us
what we really want.
Prayer also harnesses
the help of the universal energy
to aid us in our quest.

Pray for what you really want to be
and for the life you really want to live.
Pray for relief from troubles.
Pray for healing of pain.
Pray for help.
Pray to give thanks for help received.
Pray for your needs.
Pray in gratitude for what you are given.

Prayer helps free us
to overcome any limitations
we have accepted or set
for ourselves.

Praise Each Achievement

When we are teaching a child or a pet,
we reward each small effort with copious praise.

Treat yourself as a learner again.
Congratulate yourself for every small step
you take in the direction you wish to go,
toward the person you want to be
or the life you want to live.
Give yourself a kiss, a hug, a pat on the back.
Give yourself an award.
Celebrate every success, however small.

Every time you make a decision
and follow through with action,
you are creating success.
Even the mundane things
such as getting out of bed,
taking a shower,
and going to work
are successes
when you see them as steps
towards the achievement of your desires.
Every time you make a small positive change
in yourself or your life, you are creating success.
Small steps add up.
One success will lead to another.
Before you know it,
you're taking bigger steps
and achieving bigger successes.

No matter how small
or seemingly insignificant,
every desire which is followed up with action is a success!
Congratulations!

Smile, You're a Star!

As you make the changes in yourself and your life that will point you towards your desired goals, you're going to really start feeling like a success. That's great-because you are a success!

Smile like the star you are!
Smile at your face in the mirror.
Smile at others.
Your success is not at anyone else's expense;
it's good and it's right.
You deserve it fully.

So now you can afford to share
your happiness around.
Encourage others as well as yourself
with your enthusiasm.
Make it your habit
to offer positive and uplifting comments to others.
Find things to compliment and enthuse about.
Look for things for which you are grateful.
Look for things for which you are thankful.
Become a Yipee! person.
Success is all about getting what you want by your own efforts.
When your achievements
result from your own personal efforts,
you'll be rewarded with an increase
in your self-esteem and your self-confidence.
This is the real prize.

So be an inspiration
to the supporting cast in your movie.
Be a guiding star (not a prima donna).

Love, Laugh, and Live!

Love yourself and your life.
Also cherish something or someone else.
Love another person, a pet, a plant, a worthy cause.
This is for your benefit.
It's also an important part of the healing process.

Your body manufactures its own chemicals, according to your
emotional state. It is the giving of love that benefits our well-being.
When you feel loving and happy,
your body makes happy chemicals.
When you are unhappy,
it makes unhappy chemicals.
When you use drugs
that offer quick, artificial relief,
your body stops manufacturing its own
chemicals and you are left dependent
on the manufactured substitute.
So help your body to help you
by giving it every occasion
to naturally express love and joy.

Laugh as often as you can!
A good belly laugh is the best medicine possible.
Hire comedy movies.
Watch baby animals and children at play.
Tell jokes.
Slide down slippery dips.
Stomp in puddles.
Cultivating a capacity for fun
from simple pleasures will help you cope
with anything life throws at you.

Love and laughter
have even been known to cure terminal diseases,
so help yourself to wellness!

Love Unconditionally

*Do you ever hear yourself
or others say these things?
"I would love you if ..."
"I will love you when..."*

*This is conditional love.
Separate the person from the behaviour,
especially with children.
Reassure them that they are loved.
Unconditional love is total acceptance
without conditions.*

*Unconditional love
offers safety to our loved ones.
We all need to know that we are loved
even when we are at our worst.
Acceptance that we are made up
of both good and bad
and positive and negative
is the basis of commitment.
Even nature can be both cruel and kind.
The sun can nurture... or burn.
Water can save the thirsty
... or drown them.*

*It is the giving of love
that benefits our well-being.
Give your love
because it ensures your health and
happiness. Any expectation of payment from others
who receive our love will only lead to bitterness and resentment.
Loving ourselves means we are never dependent
on another for our total well-being.
Our love for ourselves can never be taken from us.*

*We can heal our own heart's pain
by loving ourselves and others
unconditionally now!*

Express Goodwill

Offer help to others.
By giving to others, we give to ourselves.
Goodwill is not something to be saved
for Christmastime;
it is a practice that can enrich our daily life experience.
It is empowering!

Try practicing acts of kindness
by offering help where you see a need for it. Volunteer for a charity,
have a pet or mind one, plant something, or start a community garden.
Try joining a program to help children in trouble. Offer to visit patients
at the local hospitals, orphanages, or aged care homes.

Bestow your goodwill on others
with your smiles and cheery greetings.
Be polite in traffic.
Be polite and positive to those with whom you work.
Pick up rubbish when you see it
and put it in the bin.
Take yours away with you
instead of leaving it lying around.
Be a good neighbour and friend
to those in your immediate environment.
Respect the feelings of yourself and others.
Express your empathy and support
to those in difficulties.

There are many ways
you can express and share goodwill sincerely.
If you share goodwill with the world,
goodwill always comes back to you too.

Take Steps to Meet Your Own Needs

We must meet our own core needs.
Feeling loved and valued
is something that must depend on your own actions,
or else you will always be at the mercy of another.
That power and responsibility is yours.

To give fully, you must give to yourself first.
When you have given to yourself first,
it is then easy to give to others
without resentment or drain.
Otherwise,
you can find yourself on the road to bitterness
from over-giving to others,
or disappointment from the expectation of return from
others for what you have given them.

If you find yourself running around and doing
for others what they could do
or learn to do for themselves, set limits.
Learn to say no.
Don't expect to burden others
with your needs either.
Taking responsibility for your own life
means avoiding unhealthy dependencies.
People will also treat you as you allow them to,
so make it your resolve
to be neither a doormat nor a doorbell.

Being an adult
means taking responsibility for yourself.
Setting limits shows respect for yourself and others.
Help others,
but also help them to help themselves.

Build Your Confidence! It's Just Like Lego!

Confidence is something we build for ourselves.
Think of any and all the successes
you've ever achieved.
A success is found when you finish a course.
It can be when you obtain a job.
It can be when you move out of home
and pay your own way.
It can be when you make new friends.
It can be when you save up the money
for something you really wanted.

Which successful changes have you made
that gave you courage?
What have you already changed
for the better about yourself or your life?
Congratulations! You're a success!

Think of times when you've stood up for yourself, held your ground,
negotiated a win-win compromise or agreement,
or settled an argument.
Congratulations! You're a success!

Think of times you've asked for something
like an extension of time on a bill,
a pay rise, or some sort of assistance,
and received it.
Congratulations! You're a success!

Think of nice things people have said about you. Think about
compliments you've received. Think about awards, rewards, and
thanks you've been given for things you've done.
Congratulations! You're a success!

Small successes add up.
All these things add to our confidence
to be more, do more, have more,
and give more.

Create Your Own Security

Security means different things to different people. It can be physical,
financial, or emotional security. We have different needs
and different levels of security.

If what is holding you back
is the dependence on another
to provide for you in some area,
take steps to change it.
Regain control.
Independence is freedom!

A rented studio flat is still your own space,
even though it's not a palace.
A job may not be the one you'd like to stay in,
but it provides money.
Good friendships and social contact
through clubs or support groups
provide nurturing, company, and support. If you are substance
dependant,
you could join a detox program
or support group.

Start somewhere.
Start anywhere to make the changes you desire
and grow from there.
Take steps that you are comfortable with;
it doesn't have to be one giant leap,
if that would scare you silly or put you off changing.

Give yourself the security you need.
Do whatever will enable you
to be your own person
and have control of your own life.

Develop Passion!

Do you have something you really want to achieve?
Do you have a goal, a vision, or a dream?

What would have you leaping out of bed
in the morning
with a smile on your face
and a song in your heart?
What do you really want to do or be?

It is the strength of your desire
that will give you the determination, focus,
and patience to persevere in achieving your goals,
manifesting your vision,
and making your dreams come true.

When you are in your right groove,
doing your main thing, and being your real self,
then you will know why you are here! This is the path to your pinnacle
of personal success, your ultimate fulfillment.

Achieving any of our desires
depends on their power of attraction.
How much we want them
will determine what we are willing to do
to achieve them.
Then simply focus,
resolve, persevere,
and be patient.

Take aim
and fire away!
You will achieve
whatever you really want to.

Understand Cravings and Addictions

Sometimes we find ourselves overly involved
in one interest or activity
to our detriment.
It may be drugs, alcohol, gambling,
making money, eating, shopping, or even exercise!

Somewhere in our unconscious,
we have negated another need.
Instead of giving some time and energy
to each of a number of needs in a balanced way,
we have put too much emphasis on one need alone.
We have overbalanced.
We have fallen down.

We have many clever ways
of justifying things to ourselves,
as well as denying what we know must be true.
Sometimes we are simply unaware
what our real needs are,
or we don't believe they can or will be met.
Our own intuition can help us get in touch
with our real needs,
as can meditation, counselling, and workshops.

Often, discovering what we really need
-love, affection, intimacy, respect, appreciation, safety,
freedom, comfort, self-expression, power
and taking steps to fulfill that need
is enough to help us give up a previous addiction.

Find Your Centre

Do you find you push yourself forward
or hold yourself back?
Maybe you do both at different times
or in different areas of your life.
Sometimes when we are reacting
or interacting with another,
we feel inclined to respond to them with an equal and opposite
reaction. We confront and conflict,
rather than consider and conciliate.

When we are centred and balanced within,
we simply state our position
and stand our ground
with an open mind and an open heart.
We are then free to objectively assess our situation, as well as
determine an appropriate course of action that does not come from a
habitual, reactive, or instinctual pattern.

Start by improving your physical balance.
Imagine walking a plank or tightrope.
Try bicycling, gymnastics, skating, skiing, surfing, Tai Chi,
or other martial arts.
Finding our physical centre of gravity
teaches us balance in every other area of our lives.
When we are centred,
we are free to remember our goals and purpose.
When we are centred, we are able to direct ourselves
towards those rewards.

Practise Equilibrium

Sometimes in order to overcome
a previous way of being,
we overbalance in the other direction.
We overcompensate.
This is all part of the learning experience.
It's nothing to be embarrassed about.
If you were learning to ride a bicycle,
you would lean one way and then the other.
You would seesaw and wobble.
You would fall and get up again.
You would do all of these things
until you learned your point of equilibrium,
your balance.

If you have been too compliant,
you may find yourself acting quite despotic at first!
If you have been unable to stand up for yourself, you may find yourself
being confrontational,
even when it's not called for.
Perhaps you felt too responsible towards others
and suddenly find yourself acting irresponsibly.
This overbalance is normal and understandable
as you strive for equilibrium.
It's a case of over and under,
a little more and a little less.
Life is about making mistakes,
learning, and correcting
to discover wholeness and equilibrium.
Life is a balancing act.
It does require flexibility.

Equalise Giving and Receiving

We breathe in and out; the tides ebb and flow;
the sun rises and sets. Life is full of opposites.

We need to honour
both our active and passive qualities,
our ability to assertively go out
and get what we want
and our ability to sit back
and graciously receive what we want.

Many of us are raised with an ethic
that supports either-but not both together.
For example,
some men are encouraged to be go-getters,
and women to be cherished.
Some women are raised to give their all for love,
and some men to be waited on hand and foot.
The path to fulfilment and balance
is in the equal honouring of giving and receiving.

Many of us also are frightened
by sadness, sorrow, loss,
and other "downers" in our lives.
Yet we accept that night follows day,
and winter is different from summer.
We need to accept and honour all opposites,
knowing that each has its time and place.
The universe is cyclic, and so are our lives.

We can consciously choose
healthy equality and balance.

We Change, Reality Doesn't

Reality simply is;
it is our perception of it that changes
according to our culture, character,
past experiences, moods, and expectations.

Different people can experience
the same event quite differently.
We can as well, when we are in
different frames of mind or states of emotion.
It is very important to realise
that things look very different to us
from the way they actually are.
The movie of life still plays,
whether we stay or leave,
and it is supremely indifferent to our reactions to it.

We are in charge of our perceptions and reactions.
We filter, analyse, and assess
what's going on out in the world,
according to what's going on inside us
and our previous experiences.
We are not objective creatures; we are human.
That is why it is best to make no long-term decisions when we are in a
low mood. Moods pass, and things look different again.
If your low mood doesn't lift, seek professional help.

Our growth is a product of change.
We can raise our awareness and choose understanding to change our
perceptions.

Create Prosperity

How we treat others
is a reflection of what we think of ourselves.
So too, our relationship with money is a reflection of our relationship
with ourselves.

When we have emotional issues
that are unacknowledged and unhealed,
we often tend to act them out
in other areas of our lives-
whether towards other people
or towards money and possessions.

Our relationship with money, for example,
is a good indicator of our emotional state.
If we fail to acknowledge our need for love,
we may try to compensate by grasping for money.
Worrying about not having enough money
shows us that we are feeling worried
about being alone and unloved.
Fear of poverty is fear of emotional abandonment.
Stinginess is fear of intimacy.
The same principle applies to material goods.
Wanting a bigger home or better car than the Joneses
shows us that we need to work on our
self-esteem and self-acceptance.
Use words to express your feelings and heal them.

By taking time and understanding
to work through our blockages,
we improve our ability
to create true prosperity and satisfaction.

Understand Friends and Enemies

As we journey through life,
we will most likely interact
with a broad variety of people.
We will find differences of gender, age, culture,
nationality, experience,
upbringing, and lifestyle;
of physical, emotional,
intellectual, or spiritual emphasis;
of morality, values, and so on.

Each of these elements
affects the way people act and interpret.
Communicating can therefore be a challenge!
It is, however, a valuable tool
that allows us to reveal who we are
and how we see the world,
as well as enabling us to learn about others.
It allows us to release energy
that gets locked up in our bodies.
It assists us to understand and be understood-
the greatest desire of all human beings.

Life is a relationship game,
and often our quality of life depends
on how well we communicate and relate to others.
Conflict, discord, and disharmony
are mostly the result of intolerance
or misunderstanding.

Our worlds are different
because our perceptions are so different.
Strive to cultivate tolerance and an open mind,
suspending all judgement
and accepting others' differences
as part of their individuality.

Understand Us and Them

*What we don't like in others
is a reflection
of what we don't accept
or acknowledge in ourselves.
When you see it as simply something
you choose not to express,
understanding comes, and acceptance
that we are all composed of the same elements
with differing emphasis
on which elements are dominant.*

*We are all made
from the same chemicals and elements,
mixed in differing combinations.
We all contain every characteristic
as well as its opposite.
For example, we are all good and bad,
introverted as well as extraverted,
independent and cooperative,
emotional, intellectual, and physical.*

*Our individuality, our natural inclinations
determine which characteristics
we will naturally express.
We can also choose to change what we express,
to become what we want to be.
The study of astrology and numerology
can help give greater understanding
of ourselves and others,
of the influences that determine
why we are the way we are.
Our time of birth
and even the energy of our names
are strong influences on us.*

We are all expressing our own individuality.

Own Your Shadow

The journey to wholeness
includes the willingness
to discover and own our shadow.
Within the context of our relationships
with friends and intimates,
we often seek those who embody characteristics
we believe we lack.
In truth, we lack for nothing.
These characteristics
were not our natural inclination,
were not encouraged,
or we were socialised out of expressing these traits while young.

Our shadow self is neither good nor bad.
Rather, it is those parts of ourselves
that we need to acknowledge
in order to achieve balance and wholeness.
When we find ourselves in conflict with others,
it is always a reflection of conflict within ourselves.
When we deny the validity of any characteristic,
we are disowning it within ourselves.
This gives rise to power struggles,
because we won't accept that we are also capable
of that of which we accuse others
(being messy, stingy, tardy, lazy, nasty).

Rather than running away from conflicts,
work through them.
Carefully examine the issues and the characteristics that annoy and irritate you.
Acknowledge and integrate yourself into wholeness.

Understand Fear

Fear is lack of belief in your own power.
It is lack of belief in your ability
to meet your own needs.
It is hopelessness and helplessness.
Fear is believing that you need to have total control over
everyone and everything that happens,
so that there are no unknowns
with which you must deal.

Face your fears fearlessly!
Why do you hesitate between desire and action?
What holds you back?
Do you fear you'll fail,
be rejected, be disliked, misunderstood?
Is it really life or death?
What is the worst result that could really happen?
If you are in danger, remove yourself quickly.
If not danger, then is your fear
that someone might say no,
or you might not get what you want?
Then you have an opportunity
to try something else,
open a dialogue, explain yourself,
reassess your goals.

You see, whatever happens,
you can and will handle it.
You will only learn your own capabilities
by using them.
You will only develop and grow
by exploring possibilities,
by living life on your feet.

Feel your fears, but empower yourself with action!

Understand Control

We have both a soul and an ego.
The soul operates on the spiritual plane,
the ego on the emotional plane.
What we often refer to as fear
is really our ego-driven efforts to keep us safe
from perceived emotional hurts and slights.

Fear of failure, fear of loss,
fear of not having, being, or doing
is how the ego drives us
to pursue ways of protecting ourselves
against perceived possible damage.
Our ego seeks to control
our environment and circumstances
in order to protect our limitations,
inadequacies, and weaknesses.

Our soul, on the other hand,
seeks to heal our inadequacies;
to assist us in raising our own self-esteem, confidence,
trust, and faith in ourselves
so that we are no longer threatened
by external events.
We are then safe and in control of ourselves;
we are able to deal with issues and events
as they arise.

Our ego's purpose is to feel our desires,
to tell us what would give pleasure and happiness. Our soul makes us
whole, so that there is nothing in us which can be hurt;
nothing that needs protection.

Trust or Bust

As you grow in self-love and understanding,
you will find that trust becomes less of an issue.
Instead of placing your trust in others,
you begin to trust yourself more.
You trust your ability to handle
whatever comes your way.
Take steps to increase your level of discernment. Trust your intuition to
warn you of those who are likely to betray you.
Take steps to protect yourself
from a betrayal of trust
by limiting your initial exposure.
Move by degrees; take small steps.
Test the waters thoroughly
before jumping in headfirst.

Take healthy precautions rather than protections;
exercise your discernment.
Often we perceive actions by others
to be a betrayal of us,
when they were only being true to themselves.
Therefore, those more likely to be trustworthy
are those whose goals, values, and
expectations resonate with our own;
those with whom there is no conflict of interest. Trust also that the outcome of
any venture results in growth.

Eliminate misunderstandings by openly discussing values, goals, and
expectations-yours and theirs.

Understand Rage and Revenge

*Rape, revenge, and other acts of intimidation and violence against
another individual are self-hatred acted out.
The "enemy" is perceived by the perpetrator
as a non-person; not human,
and by this method,
they are able to justify
their actions to themselves.*

*Obviously, the qualities of empathy and acceptance
for themselves and others
are sadly lacking in these individuals.
If you are faced with such a person or situation
and are unable to remove yourself,
try offering empathy, acceptance, and friendship.
Refuse to accept or mirror their hate.
Stay calm.*

*Sometimes a comment such as,
"You must have had a bad day/time/life"
can be enough to catch them off guard
and defuse their hate.
When you are offering
friendship and understanding,
it becomes more difficult for them to hold you out
as the enemy.
By introducing human qualities,
you can succeed
in rehumanising the dehumanisation
necessary for acting out self-hate.*

*By offering unconditional care,
concern, and safety to others,
we ensure it for ourselves.*

Understand Despair, Depression, and Desperation

Depression is our ego's response
when we feel totally overwhelmed
by our inability to control our environment. Through our ego, we
perceive ourselves to be powerless to effect change;
to achieve this would require change
in everything or everyone involved
except ourselves.

When we want reality to change,
it is our ego that drives this desire.
Sometimes we fall into despair
because we don't get the particular partner,
job, or house we want.
We become attached to the object of our desire.
This can lead to desperation,
because we don't trust in our growth process.

When we shift our focus back to our original desire,
we see the description, the qualities and details,
rather than that particular object.
This is our soul helping us to know
that there are many choices for us,
many options that will fulfil our desires.
Our soul heals our ego's pain; our soul sets us free.

Everything and everyone is in our life for a reason,
but not always meant to stay.
When it's really right for you,
you will be right for it too.

Life Is Like a Spiral

Have you noticed that things repeat?
Experiences you have been through before
come around again,
and sometimes again and again.

Every experience contains a lesson.
Until we learn that lesson,
the experience will helpfully repeat for us.
We attract these experiences
in order to learn about ourselves
and to find and fix our problems.

If we can extract the lesson from the experience, learn from it, and
move on, we will find ourselves moving forward
to better experiences, richer for the learning
we have gained.
Onwards and upwards!

Sometimes the experience can be very painful.
Truly living life means we will know pain
as well as happiness, sorrow as well as joy.
We can't really appreciate one
until we have an understanding of its opposite.
We become whole by experiencing
the entire range of life experiences:
the ups and downs, the good and the bad.

In order to grow and change,
we need to experience and learn.

Life is a course in living.

Rejection Is Not a Put-Down, It's a Blessing

When your partner leaves you, you lose your job,
or you are rejected in some way,
do you take it personally,
decide you are in the wrong,
and turn it into self-hatred?

We often perceive criticism and rejection
where none exists.
We then allow it to poison us.
Why?
The reality is quite different.

To find the right partner,
career, or lifestyle,
we need to find out what's not right.
This is the case for others as well.
Just because we are not right for a particular one
doesn't mean we are wrong for all!
Freeing ourselves from the wrong one
means we are then available for the right one!

Put things in their proper perspective;
when looking for what we like
in clothing or accessories, homes, or cars,
we try many options to find what's right for us.
We easily let go of the ones we don't want,
those that aren't right for us.
It's the same with people and partners.

When we love ourselves,
we say no to what's not right for us
and allow others the same choice.

Practise Respectful Farewells

Sometimes when we grow and change,
we find that others currently in our lives
don't grow with us.
We can grow apart and in different directions.

This can happen with long-term relationships, friendships, jobs,
even cultures and neighbourhoods.

A major change in our lives is like a rebirth,
and every rebirth contains an element of death.
The old you, the person you used to be, has moved on.
Sometimes we need to say good-bye
to more than just outgrown clothes.
We may experience sadness and loss,
but change is necessary for growth.

There is nothing bad or wrong with others
who are unwilling or unable to change
and grow with us.
We had that experience for a reason.
If it was not a positive experience,
we will have gained something from it,
even if it's only learning what we don't want!

A calm and mature farewell
and best wishes for the other's future,
moving on with gratitude and thanks
for what we have had, shared, or learned with them,
will ensure a better future for all involved.

Growth through Relationship

*It is virtually impossible to reach adulthood
without being wounded in some way, unintentionally or not, during
our formative years.*

*We all, therefore, feel incomplete in some way
and are looking for our "other half"
to make us whole.
Our choices in relationships are good for us
when they challenge us to work through the process of growth into
wholeness.
We seek to get, but it is giving that heals us.
Our choice of partner is determined
by our true needs,
those which lead to our growth.*

*We are challenged to stretch ourselves
towards wholeness
through meeting our partner's needs.
Ultimately, we develop those qualities
of "our other half" within ourselves.
Healing our own wounds is thus effected,
however difficult we may find this process.
Our partner, in turn,
is going through a similar process on our behalf
for his or her equal benefit.
Commitment allows us
to weather conflict and grow.*

*It is our giving of love,
commitment, and companionship
that ultimately leads to our healing,
growth, and fulfilment.*

What Is True Love?

Our choice of life partner
is one of the most important decisions
we will ever make.

This is the person
who will share our most intimate relationship,
who will interact with us on a daily basis,
and who will have the greatest effect
and influence on us.

Intimate relationships are healthiest
when they are equal.
In other words, when both partners
respect and appreciate each other,
decisions are mutually agreed upon,
and both take responsibility
for the success of the partnership.
Strong relationships are pleasurable
and satisfying for both parties,
meeting their respective needs in a
manner that enriches their life experience.

If your relationship
has communication and commitment,
friendship and shared interests,
common values and goals,
compatibility and caring,
enjoyment of each other's company
and mutual desire,
you are blessed
with one of life's most pleasurable
and rewarding experiences-true love.

Soul Mates

We feel attraction for others on different levels.
We have relationships that are physical,
emotional, intellectual,
or any combination of the above.

Your soul mate, however,
is the one who sees and reflects your soul.
When you meet your own needs,
you are free to share yourself with another,
simply because
he or she is the one you want to be with.
There is no obligation, no expectation;
you are together for the purpose of sharing yourself and your journey
with another.

Your soul mate is not a mirror image of you;
rather, the experiences and differences
this individual brings to you
enable you to be more of what you really are.
The interaction between your souls
frees you to expand
into the totality of your respective beings.

We can have different soul mates
for different areas of our life.
To attract your soul mate,
you don't posture or pose,
manipulate or deceive.
You simply offer yourself
as a genuine, radiant being
and glow like a beacon.
As such, you are divinely irresistible
to your soul mate.

Heal Yourself

Time cures all ills.
Yes, it does-but that is not the whole story.
Often, time fades the memory,
but the wound is still there,
festering or calloused.

To achieve healing and wholeness,
we need awareness
of the why, the how, and the what.
Why is it so, how did it happen,
and what was it about?
We learn about ourselves
in the practical laboratory of life.
We learn what our beliefs are.

The common denominator in all our problems, trials,
and tribulations is not them but us.
When we take steps
to discover why things happen to us
and how we came to hold certain beliefs
and what those beliefs are;
healing can take place,
and new wounds can be avoided entirely.

Often we choose our experiences unconsciously
to confirm what we believe to be true
about ourselves.
With awareness, we can change our beliefs
and therefore change our experiences.
As we understand, we heal.

Healing is not an event;
it is the dawning of realisation,
the awakening of awareness.

Change Requires Patience

When we plant a seed in the garden,
its growth is not visible immediately.
The same is true of any growth or change.

First to grow are the roots below the surface.
Only when the roots are firmly established
can the visible growth commence.
The foundations or base must come first,
in order to support the new structure.

The first stage is the planting of the seed;
the second stage is the germination;
and finally comes the harvest.
As roots grow in the darkness underground,
so our soul's growth is achieved
during the dark periods of our lives.
All growth and change occurs
first in the invisible world.
By the time it becomes visible,
it is already almost complete.

So take heart!
Patiently await the magnificent fruit of your efforts to change and
grow beyond your previous limits. Follow the process in good faith,
knowing that behind the scenes,
change is taking place,
and success is coming to you.

It may not happen overnight, but I happen.

Cultivate Your Garden

Think of your mind, body, and life
in terms of a garden.
What exactly do you want to grow?

Careful attention and awareness
will ensure that your garden grows
the way you want it to!
Weed out those opinions, attitudes, and habits
that are taking up the space
you would rather fill with the beautiful flowers
of joyful thoughts and deeds.

Fertilize your soil with affirmations,
loving care, and other good nutrients.
Carefully prune the overgrowth of excesses
with gentleness,
and support the shrubs of your dreams and goals
in their early stages,
to ensure they grow tall and strong.
Surround your garden with a protective border,
that all may enjoy its beauty
without trampling over the blooms
and knocking down the shrubs.
Use natural methods to control bugs, and water your garden deeply
with faith, so the roots may grow strong enough to withstand an
occasional drought.
Take pleasure in the process of creating
and equal pleasure in harvesting
the fruits of your labour.
When you sow love, you reap love.

Change Your Patterns

We need to complete our transformation
with new ways of being who we are
and new tools to get what we want.
Whilst we can make many positive changes
in our lives quickly; effective changes to our patterns and our
behaviour habits requires time, practice and repetition.

We now know that we are responsible
for everything we think, feel, and do.
We now set personal boundaries
to allow ourselves time and space for our own needs. We respect and
express ourselves assertively,
in our best interests.
We have friendships
with supportive, positive people.
We are supportive, positive people.
We have understanding of ourselves and others.
We choose to focus on the good in life.

We say no to unreasonable demands.
We say what we feel without blaming another;
we trust ourselves.
We know our power to meet our own needs
and ask for help directly when we need it.
We feel our power to create the life we want
and achieve our desires.

Our new behaviour reflects our new awareness
of our right to our life, happiness, and success.

Communicate Your Changes

Now we need to communicate the changes in us effectively to others.

When we find our own power,
we are no longer victims
who are too accommodating, too easily influenced
or unable or unwilling to stand up for ourselves. Neither do we need to
protect ourselves against others by manipulation, coercion, avoidance,
control, or trying to change them.

Practice small steps.
Don't automatically agree to something
you may not want to do.
Allow others to do the same.
Use dialogue; use assertive words
which state your position:
I think … I feel … I'd like to …
I don't like it when you …
Be direct.

Use power, not protection.
In this way, you will find respect, cooperation,
and harmony in your relations with others.
Practice right relations with yourself and others.
Be assertive instead of passive-aggressive, controlling,
or manipulative.

Remember, it's not what they do;
it's what we let them do to us
and what we do to ourselves.

Be a Human Being

We are called human beings, not human doings. What you are, the you
that directs your thoughts and actions, is a being.
It is the being who directs the doing.

Heal, nurture, and expand the being you are.
Even if you achieve this by doing,
do not lose sight of the being.
Be strong yet gentle; be wise but also light-hearted;
be straight yet flexible;
be relaxed yet ready to spring into action;
be adventurous but not reckless;
be at peace yet fully alive.

We are human beings, not machines.
We have the capacity to think and strategise,
to feel and react, to act morally and conscientiously, to consciously
create or destroy, to think before we act.
Be mindful in your choices;
we are each here to follow our desires to happiness, but not at
another's expense.
We all have a right to be here, to be free,
to be responsible for ourselves,
and to pursue our individual dreams.
We do not have the right to do harm
to another soul on this planet.

Treat all life, including your own,
with reverence and respect.

Understand Successful Growth

Success is sometimes a fleeting event,
a moment that passes all too quickly.
True success is a state of being.
It is the state of calm, contented fulfilment.

When we are who we want to be,
doing what we want to do
with whom we want to do it,
then we have achieved true success.
Of course, change continues, and events transpire,
whether we choose them to or not.
Losing a partner or job redundancy
is not a conscious choice for us,
but in the larger scheme of things,
it does not mean the end of our success.
It is only the end of that particular success.
We can go on and create another success
with different elements-
a new partner, a new career, a new life, a new self.

Success happens when we allow ourselves
to be the best we can be.
We are at peace with ourselves and our world.
We allow soul and spirit to guide us,
and as such are in harmony with all creation.

We don't have to accept the stereotypes
of growing up or growing old.
Rather, real success
is growing into the wholeness of you!

Use Life Skills

To really live in this world requires life skills.
We can learn these skills by trial and error,
or we can learn from those who have gone before us.

Often, those who become parents,
those who take on the job of teaching us,
are completely unaware and unprepared
through lack of knowledge or healing themselves. Unknowingly, they
can pass on their woundedness to their children.
As adults, we are therefore often faced
with the task of unlearning
much of what we were taught.
If we can be healed before we become parents,
so much the better for the next generation.

If individuals can be healed, then society is healed, and the world
ultimately becomes better for us all. We are all entrusted with the
care of each other; that is what society is about.
Living life requires responsibility as well as freedom.

Life really is a wonderful experience.
Good life skills
can make your experience superlative.

You do have the power to heal the world,
just by healing yourself.

Express the God-ness Within

The power of one is the power you have
to make a difference in the world
during your time here.

When you allow your higher self, your soul,
to guide your thoughts, desires, and actions,
not only is your life experience transcendental,
but your impact on the world
is also of a much higher calibre.

Your soul becomes aware of its own greatness
as you raise your consciousness.
When you know you are the creator
of your own life, you see the God within yourself.
As God is the Creator of the world,
we are the creators of our world.
We also have the power of creation,
the greatness and the goodness that is God.
This is what is meant by the saying
that we are created in God's image-his spirit image.

As God allows us, we allow ourselves and others
to have freedom of choice, to live by discernment, not judgement, to
honour all life, because if it exists, it is expressing God.
We express our love for ourselves and others.
We are united in mind, body, and soul.

We are whole, as well as part of the whole.

Cherish the God-ness Without

Our planet is a marvel!
It gives freely of its pleasures and treasures,
that we may live and flourish.

Our planet gives us clean air to breathe,
grass under our feet,
rich soil to grow our fruits and vegetables,
trees to make oxygen,
and plants to heal our ailments
and refresh our souls with their beauty.
Our planet truly offers us everything we need
for our well-being.

We have the free will to either preserve or destroy our natural
heritage and bounty. We can choose to work with nature,
in harmony with her ways-or against her.
Our materialistic society is causing an increase
in disease and disharmony
in those it professes to serve.
We have created this society,
and we can therefore also choose
to create a different one.
We are only just rediscovering
that we are destroying
what nature has provided with love,
endangering our own survival in the process.

Our future survival is in our own hands.
What kind of future do you want?

Achieve Cosmic Wholeness

Cosmic wholeness is the achievement
of oneness with the universe.
It is the awareness of ourselves and our impact
in relation to the whole of creation.

It is the recognition
that there are no strangers in this world,
only friends we haven't yet met.
It is the love and care that we show for all,
as the natural expression of a joy-filled life.
It is the embracing of all life's experiences,
recognising the purpose each has
for our growth and evolution.
It is living to the fullest,
yet with peace and tranquillity.
It is thriving on the challenge of adversity,
knowing that it contains the potential for triumph.

It is detachment,
in that we are of the world but not mired in it.
It is the acceptance, kindness, and patience
we give to all, including ourselves, as we grow.
It is inner strength, not brittleness.
It is flowing with the cyclic nature of things,
knowing that change is the only constant.

It is aliveness. It is passion.
It is balance and harmony.
It is living multidimensionally.

Achieve Regeneration

We have learned much in our shared journey
to achieving regeneration and wholeness!

We have come to a maturity in our develoment, where we can
welcome each adversay as a challenge and each difficullty
as a learning experience.

We no longer blame circumstances
or others for determining our lives.
Rather, we use them to shape our growth.
We have found our centre,
the source of power, within ourselves.
We are no longer victims;
we have control of ourselves and our lives.
We take responsibility
for creating our own experiences, our own destiny.
We are guiltless and blamesless.

Our lives are in order,
in harmony with the universe at large.
We have found our right place.
We have achieved a clear vision
of what we want and what we must do
to achieve our vision of the future.

We are in touch with our true nature-
simple, direct, loving, feeling,
and able to touch the stars,
even as our feet remain firmly on the ground.

We are truly alive!

Completion

My rose seeks the sun,
The good and the true.
My rose seeks the light,
Its bloom to renew.

My rose, it has lived,
And learned about life.
My rose seeks peace and harmony,
Not trouble and strife.

My rose is strong yet supple.
It bends but survives.
No storm can break my rose-
If damaged, it revives.

And after each storm,
The sun shines again,
Giving warmth and nurturing
To heal any pain.

-Joelle Lewis

Suggested Authors for Further Reading

Dale Carnegie

Mihaly Csikszentmihalyi

Dr. Richard Carlson

Dr. Wayne Dyer

Clarissa Pinkola Estes

Shakti Gawain

Kahlil Gibran

Dr. John Gray

Louise Hay

Paul Hanna

Dr. Harville Hendrix

Jean Housten

Susan Jeffers

M. Scott Peck

Catherine Ponder

Dr. Maxwell Maltz

Michael Domeyko Rowland

Anthony Robbins

Barbara Sher

Robert A. Schuller

Joan Sotkin

Barbara and Terry Tebo

I wish to acknowledge and thank the above authors for their help and assistance in my journey.

About the Author

Joelle Lewis grew up in Wahroonga, a glorious, tree-filled area of the North Shore in Sydney, Australia. As a child, she loved animals and nature, held a firm belief that the universe was an intelligent and loving entity, dreamed, drew pictures of horses, and wrote copious amounts of poetry.

Through her many adventures and challenges, Joelle has connected deeply with a wide variety of people and experienced many different ways of living.

Joelle's books reflect her understanding and awareness, her empathy for all souls, as well as her passion and love for life, which enabled her to pick herself up after traumatic experiences, heal, and move on to far better experiences, deeper joy, and a richer life. Her suggested healing methods are holistic, integrating both mainstream and alternative methodologies.

Joelle is also the author of I'm Going to Give Myself Some Very Good Advice... and Then I'm Going to Take It!